Original title:
The Sweetest Strawberries

Copyright © 2025 Creative Arts Management OÜ
All rights reserved.

Author: Mariana Leclair
ISBN HARDBACK: 978-1-80586-358-8
ISBN PAPERBACK: 978-1-80586-830-9

Blissful Harvest Moon

Under the moon, we skip and sway,
Juicy tales of harvest play.
Berries bounce, so full of glee,
Who knew fruit could be so free?

Laughter echoes, oh what a sight,
Their red cool suits are pure delight.
We'll juggle them with sticky hands,
Nature's candy, oh how it stands!

A Dance of Flavor and Light

In fields where giggles bloom like seeds,
Taste buds twirl for fruity needs.
A waltz of sweetness, bright and bold,
These treasures, worth their weight in gold.

Surprise inside, like a silly joke,
Lemonade dreams with a berry poke.
We dance and munch in joyous streams,
With fruity frolics that fill our dreams!

Ruby Gems on Green Canvas

Amidst the leaves, bright jewels shine,
A treasure hunt, oh how divine!
Rubies rest on nature's quilt,
With every bite, our cares are spilt.

Fumble fingers, oh what a mess,
A berry splash can't be suppressed!
A giggle here, a squirt right there,
Who knew fruit fight could bring such flair?

Charm of the Sun-drenched Orchard

In sunlit fields, we wander free,
With nectar dreams, just you and me.
A harvest dance of joy unbound,
Sweet chaos in the orchard found.

Red crowns on our heads, we parade,
As laughter echoes, fears do fade.
A berry fling, the silliest game,
We'll forever cherish this sweet fame!

Joy Bursting in Every Berry

In the garden where giggles bloom,
Chubby fruits tease with a berry boom.
Each bite a burst, a cheeky surprise,
Winking at us with fruity eyes.

Picked by critters in a sneaky race,
They laugh and dance, oh what a chase!
A splash of red in the green parade,
Nature's candy, hilarity made.

A Harvest of Hidden Treasures

Under leaves where secrets lie,
Little red jewels catch the eye.
Some are plump, while others shrink,
Like cousins who forgot to drink.

In baskets they tumble, a jolly crew,
Squeezing up squabbles on what to chew.
Each round bite paints a goofy grin,
As laughter spills where the fun begins.

Sweetness Woven in Silence

In whispers soft, the berries grow,
Quietly plotting their sweet show.
A sugar rush on the sneaky side,
While squirrels giggle in a fruity ride.

Under stars, they spin their tales,
As crickets sing their fruity scales.
Touched by dew and moonbeams bright,
These little gems bring pure delight.

Garden Gambol of Flavor

Bumbling bunnies hop and prance,
While down below, the berries dance.
One took a dive, what a weird slip!
Landing right in a jammy trip!

Picnics planned with wildly sweet
Roses giggle at each cute feat.
With every bite, a laugh we share,
In this garden full of berry flair.

Juicy Whispers of Summer

In gardens where the sun does beam,
Berries hide, like a sweetened dream.
With mud on shoes and stains on hands,
We hunt for treasure in these lands.

A sneaky squirrel steals a bite,
We laugh and chase in pure delight.
Red rubies burst with every smash,
We'll feast all day, then take a splash!

Fields of Ripe Temptation

In fields where giggles fill the air,
We munch and crunch without a care.
The sun is hot, the juice does trickle,
Each berry's tartness makes us giggle.

Oh, watch your step, there's mud aplenty,
And don't you dare bring in a dent-y!
With sticky fingers and smeared-up face,
We run around this berry space!

A Taste of Sun-kissed Joy

With baskets swinging, off we go,
To find the sweetest red on show.
Each morsel plump, a tiny fist,
Who knew "work" could feel like bliss?

The birds above sing funny tunes,
As we dive deep to find our spoons.
We taste and laugh with every bite,
A merry picnic, pure delight!

Harvest of Heartstrings

When evening falls, we gather near,
With berries bright and smiles sincere.
Our laughter mingles with the breeze,
As we all scramble for the cheese.

The tales we spin, the jokes we tell,
All mixed with juice; oh, what a spell!
A harvest full of love and cheer,
With every berry, friends draw near.

Nature's Candy in Bloom

In gardens bright, they play peekaboo,
Juicy little gems all wet with dew.
A squirrel danced, tried to steal a bunch,
But tripped on roots and went in for lunch.

Sun-kissed treasures in every bite,
A berry party, what pure delight!
We laugh so hard, the birds join along,
Nature's candy, where we all belong.

Embracing Summer's Essence

Beneath the sun, we take a seat,
With hats so large, we can't compete.
The berries laugh, they know the score,
They roll away, we chase and roar!

Red as a clown's nose, sweet and round,
Their sticky juice all over town.
We slip and slide, what a crazy day,
Summer giggles in a fruity way.

Whispering Leaves and Berry Scores

The leaves do rustle with secrets to share,
While berries gossip without a care.
They plot and scheme in the warm sunshine,
To tickle our taste buds, oh how divine!

A raccoon swoops down, looking for treats,
A berry buffet suits his grand feats.
We point and laugh as he munches with glee,
Who knew a critter could be so fancy?

Woodland Rhapsody of Blushing Fruits

In the woods where mischief runs free,
A berry decided to swing from a tree.
It got tangled up, oh what a sight,
The vines oh-so-tangled gave all a fright!

The critters gathered, a show to be seen,
With giggles and snickers, it was quite the scene.
A patch of plumpness, laughter defined,
In the heart of the woods, pure joy we find.

Echoes of Laughter in the Patch

In the patch, we trip and fall,
Muddy knees and laughter's call.
Berries burst, a vivid red,
Pies to make, but first, we're fed.

Squirrels watch with eyes so wide,
As we munch and run to hide.
Berry juice runs down our chins,
Oops! Another berry wins!

Nature's Candy and Sunlight

Sunshine beams on juicy treats,
Sugar rush from nature's feats.
Biting in with glee, we grin,
Stains of red on every skin.

A rogue berry rolls away,
Who can chase? Let's make it play!
Sour giggles fill the air,
Biscuits gone, but we don't care!

A Feast of Fragile Flavors

Tiny treasures bloom so bright,
Planting mischief feels so right.
Plates piled high with berry bliss,
We'll share a laugh and not a kiss.

Wiggly worms might steal a snack,
They've got sights, but we don't lack!
One for you and two for me,
A berry bounty, oh, so free!

Nectar of the Garden

Oh, the fields, a sight divine,
Pint-sized treasures ambrosial shine.
Fingers sticky, giggles burst,
Who knew fruit could quench our thirst?

Under bushes, we conspire,
Stealing bites so we can retire.
Nature's jewels, a playful game,
And in the end, we're all to blame!

Taste of Innocence

In a patch of berry bliss,
A dog disguised as a chef,
Squeezes fruit in a blissful mess,
Was it my pie or his stealth?

Juice drips down my chin,
Like rain from a funny cloud,
I dance around in a spin,
With laughter that sings out loud.

Savoring Sunlit Memories

Under the sun, we took a bite,
A taste that made us squeal,
Chasing each other in pure delight,
With berry juice for every meal.

We wore the stains like badges bright,
Giggling with a sticky hand,
A fruit fight in the golden light,
Was this ever really planned?

Enchanted Moments in Red

A squirrel stole my fruit-filled prize,
He winked, and off he flew,
I swear I saw him roll his eyes,
In a tasty act quite askew.

With red-stained cheeks and a silly grace,
We chased the furry thief,
A berry chase around the place,
We laughed away our grief.

Harvesting Laughter Among Leaves

In the garden, we made a pact,
To nibble and giggle, never act,
The mushy ones, we deemed a fact,
Were simply fruit love, that's how we stacked!

With every pluck, a joke was made,
Belly laughs filled the sweet parade,
No berry could escape our tirade,
As we feasted in the sunny glade.

A Basket of Wonder

In a basket they sit, plump and round,
Chasing squirrels, they make no sound.
They giggle and laugh, a little parade,
Bright red jesters, they've got it made.

Plucked from the vine, they roll on the floor,
Wobbling 'round like they're seeking more.
One took a dive, oh what a sight!
Landing in cream, what a funny delight!

Rapture in Every Bite

Biting into bliss, oh what a tease,
A giggle escapes, they aim to please.
Squirty and bright, they dance on the tongue,
Making us laugh, while we are young.

With little green hats, they wear their leaves,
A reason for joy, that's all one believes.
They may roll away in a berry fight,
Leaving us grinning, what pure delight!

Lush Treasures of the Earth

Tucked in the fields, hidden from sight,
They plot their escape, a true berry flight.
With juicy tales and sweet little schemes,
They laugh in the sun, living out dreams.

Pints piled high, a treasure of fun,
Squeezing through crates, they dash, they run.
In a pie they frolic, a pastry show,
Filling our bellies with giggles that flow!

Murmurs of Berry-bright Horizons

Whispering secrets beneath leafy beds,
Strawberries chatter, using their heads.
Plotting their sweetness, they grin cheek to cheek,
With laughter and joy, they never feel weak.

Rolling through puddles, they find such delight,
In every mishap, they twinkle so bright.
A juicy conclave with fruits on parade,
Making us chuckle; oh, how they charade!

Orchard Dreams Beyond the Horizon

In a patch where laughter grows,
Berries dance, and mischief flows.
They giggle under leafy crowns,
While teasing squirrels steal their gowns.

Sun-kissed sweetness in a jar,
One cheeky rabbit, a berry czar.
Plucking fruits while wearing shades,
Sipping juice, throwing parades.

Birds chirp tunes, quite off-key,
The harvest moon winks at me.
Pies are bubbling, dreams take flight,
In this orchard, joy ignites!

Every berry has a tale,
Of fruity jokes and happy trails.
When life gives you a berry stain,
Just wear it proud, then dance in rain.

Secret Garden of Blushing Jewels

In a garden full of giggles,
Berries blush where nature wriggles.
They wear capes of green and red,
And tease the bees who bump their head.

Sneaky raccoons come to play,
Stashing fruit in a sly ballet.
With painted rocks and secret signs,
They hoard their treasures, oh so fine!

Beneath the sun, they plot and scheme,
Dreaming big of berry cream.
Pull a berry, take a chance,
Join the critters in their dance!

A crown of leaves upon their head,
In berry land, there's never dread.
With laughter bursting, skies so blue,
In this spectacle, there's fun for you!

Nature's Palette of Flavor

A rainbow spills on grass so green,
Berries giggle, a fruity scene.
Painted in flavors, bold and bright,
They challenge tongues to a tasty fight!

With each bite, a new surprise,
Sticky fingers, happy eyes.
Splashing juice like summer rain,
Fruits tasting power, pure and plain.

Worms in sunglasses twist and twirl,
As silly seeds begin to swirl.
Nature's brush is wild and free,
Creating flavors just for me!

When the jam jar starts to jig,
You know it's time for a grand gig.
Grab a spoon, let's dig right in,
In this fruity fun, we'll surely win!

Echoes of Berry Bliss

In fields where nectar sings of cheer,
The critters gather, far and near.
Tickled toes in strawberry patches,
While ants march on, in little batches.

A hop, a skip, a berry dance,
Every berry's got a chance.
To roll away or take a stand,
With little paws across the land!

Time for fruit fights in the sun,
Splat goes the juice, oh what fun!
Smiling faces, messy clothes,
In berry lands, laughter grows!

So grab a friend and join the spree,
In this jammy jubilee.
With echoes of joy in every twist,
Berry bliss, you can't resist!

Crimson Elegy in a Field of Green

In fields of green where blushes grow,
I tripped on roots and fell, oh no!
A berry laughed, a cheeky tease,
I swore to halt my berry fees.

With juice on chin, I took a stand,
But slippery paths make rules unplanned.
A dance with dirt, a comical plight,
On hands and knees, a berry fight!

The Allure of Plump Perfection

A basket brimming, I'm on a quest,
To find that fruit I love the best.
But as I reach with berry glee,
A squirrel declares, 'That one's for me!'

I chase him round, we swirl and spin,
Our game of tag, oh where to begin?
He nibbles fast, I nibble slow,
A showdown in the berry row!

Gentle Sunbeams and Fruity Dreams

Sunshine tickles as I delight,
In little orbs that shine so bright.
I take a bite, and woeful cries,
For juice erupts, oh what a surprise!

Friends laughing hard, they can't believe,
That fruit could cause such hefty grief.
But with each squirt, comes joy anew,
I reap the giggles, berry goo!

Bountiful Moments in Bloom

In the garden, a rare sight shown,
A cheerful plant all on its own.
It waved to me as I turned back,
'Pick me first, don't lose your snack!'

With petals soft, it made its plea,
But I just laughed, 'Oh, let it be!'
Then slipped and rolled, a tumble spree,
That cheeky bloom still giggles free!

The Allure of Delicate Harvests

In the garden where giggles grow,
Berries blush in a dazzling row.
They see my basket, all aglow,
"Pick me! Pick me!" they start to crow.

Tasting tufts of ruby delight,
I snack and dance in pure delight.
Plump and round, a joyful sight,
I may just eat them all tonight!

But as I feast with eager glee,
I hear a rustle from a tree.
A squirrel eyes my bounty spree,
"Those are mine!" it shouts with glee!

Now I'm racing, quick and spry,
Me against a thief, oh my!
The berries glisten, I can't deny,
It's a berry brawl, a frantic fry!

Lively Secrets in Soft Hues

In the patch of colors bright,
Beneath the leaves, oh what a sight!
Laughter bubbles, pure delight,
As I hide for a tasty bite.

A sneaky peek, they wink at me,
"I dare you, come and see!"
With each taste, I giggle, whee!
How did I eat seven, oh gee!

Little critters join the fun,
Each nibble brings another pun.
"Share the treasure, just a one!"
But I'm in the mood to run!

Pink riches scattered all around,
In this patch, joy is profound.
With sticky fingers, I'm unbound,
In the chaos, laughter's found!

Sweetness Found Beneath Thorny Vines

Amidst the prickles, there's a thrill,
I brave the thorns, but what a spill!
Harvest dreams with every quill,
Who knew eating could be such a skill?

First a taste, then a daring race,
Nature's candy, what a chase!
I end up with a berry face,
Surrounded by my pink disgrace.

"Can you share?" the birds will plead,
I shake my head, "I'll take the lead!"
But just one more, that's my creed,
In berry bliss, I plant the seed!

With giggles ringing in the sun,
This berry battle's just begun.
Who knew such joy could come from fun?
With muddied hands, I've surely won!

Garden of Tempting Charms

In a secret spot where mischief hides,
Tiny gems play peekaboo outside.
With a laugh, I'll take a ride,
To snack and munch, they're my pride.

But oh, what's that? A twinkling sound!
A sneaky rabbit hops around.
"Hey there, friend, don't be so proud,
I want a share, let's make a crowd!"

Sticky fingers, a joyful mess,
These juicy treasures, I must confess.
In this garden, I'm truly blessed,
And in sweet chaos, I must digress.

So come and join this tasty cheer,
Let's pluck the joy from far and near.
In laughter, taste, and berry beer,
A garden party is right here!

The Color of Sweetness

In the garden, fruit so bright,
Poking fun at birds in flight.
With a wiggle and a wink,
They tease us, don't you think?

Juicy globes in every hue,
Bouncing like a lively crew.
Sun-kissed laughter, sweet appeal,
How do they manage this surreal?

Chasing critters with a grin,
Plucking one and then a twin.
Each bite bursts, oh what a game,
It's a fruit that sparks the fame!

So join the dance of tart and sweet,
Where every nibble is a treat.
Life's too short to take a seat,
Get messy, taste, enjoy, repeat!

Chaotic Harmony of Tart and Sweet

Underneath the big, blue sky,
Bouncing berries zooming by.
They argue, 'I'm more tart than you!'
While giggling in the morning dew.

With a splash of cheerful red,
Tangled vines form a funny bed.
"Don't squish me!" the green ones shout,
In this chaotic berry bout.

A pie in progress, what a sight,
Splatters everywhere — what a plight!
Who knew such delightful mess,
Could lead to such a tasty stress?

So gather 'round, let's bake some fun,
With laughter shared, we've already won.
Tart and sweet in perfect harmony,
Nothing better, can't you see?

Melody of Crimson Delight

Swinging in the summer breeze,
Berries whisper like the trees.
"Pick me first!" they loudly plead,
In their wacky berry creed.

A jam jar full of silly songs,
Debates on where each berry belongs.
One claims to be the jester's prize,
While another rolls its fruity eyes.

With every squish, a giggle flies,
As berry juice rains from the skies.
Dancing on the sunlit floor,
Life's a treat we can't ignore!

Savoring bites of pure delight,
While laughter draws the stars at night.
So let's all raise a sugary toast,
To these berries we love the most!

Solstice Serenade of Summer Fruits

Under the sun, they play and tease,
Silly fruits dance in the breeze.
"Look at me!" each one will shout,
In this radiant berry rout.

Stomping on the ripe parade,
Belly laughs that never fade.
A sprinkle of sugar, just for fun,
Making serious sweetness on the run.

Squishy giggles fill the air,
As cherries leap, they have no care.
"Take a bite!" the juicy laughs call,
A festival, delighting all!

So here's to summer and the cheer,
Flavors dancing, oh so near.
With every bite, let's unite,
In this wild and fruity flight!

Gemstones Beneath the Green

In the garden ripe with cheer,
Little fruits dance, oh so near.
Got my basket, I'll be quick,
Hiding treasures, what a trick!

Lush and bright, those gems so round,
Chasing critters all around.
Watch as I trip, oh dear me!
Nature's pranks are free, you'll see!

Each bite's a burst of sweet surprise,
Squirrels watch with hungry eyes.
Who knew berries held such glee?
Rolling down the hill with me!

But wait—my hat flew through the air!
Chasing it, I lose my flair.
A fruit just landed on my nose!
I am now the Berry Rose!

Nature's Bounty in Full Bloom

Under sun, the laughter grows,
Fruits are giggling, who really knows?
Popping up like jokes so sweet,
Nature's candy, can't be beat!

Sun hats tilting, all askew,
Picking berries, just me and you.
Stumbling over tangled vines,
Creating quite a mess of lines!

Shiny red and oh-so-loud,
Fruit brigade, I'm feeling proud.
But instead of berries bright,
I found a toad—what a fright!

In my basket, dreams come true,
Fruits and frogs, oh what a stew!
Nature's bounty, full of glee,
Let's dance, my silly berry spree!

Whispers of the Berry Harvest

Hush now, hear the whispers sweet,
Fruits are plotting their grand feat.
Rolling down the garden path,
With a chuckle, they can't help but laugh!

Sneaky fruits hiding by the stone,
They wink and giggle, not alone.
With every step, I hear them say,
"Catch us quick, before we play!"

Fingers sticky, face all smeared,
Eating them, oh dear, I'm weird!
Watch the ants join in the fun,
Dancing 'round under the sun!

Turning round, I kiss the ground,
Who knew fruits could be so round?
Each laugh's a berry, ripe and true,
Join the harvest, me and you!

Dappled Sunlight on Plump Delights

In the patch where laughter grows,
Sunlight dapples, and it shows.
Up and down, the bushes sway,
Let's have fun and eat away!

Juggling fruits, oh what a sight,
One fell down and took a bite!
"Catch me if you dare," it teases,
Rolling off like silly breezes!

Sticky fingers, giggles loud,
Wearing berry juice, feel so proud.
Mama's calling—where's my snack?
Oops, I think I lost a pack!

Bouncing berries, high and low,
Chasing them, it's quite a show!
Life is sweet, and oh so right,
With plump delights, what a delight!

The Aroma of Ruby Red

A berry slipped, oh what a mess,
It rolled away, I must confess.
Chasing it down, I lost my shoe,
Thought I'd catch it, but how it flew!

The scent it spread was quite a tease,
Attracting a swarm of buzzing bees.
I waved my arms, I danced around,
But all I caught was grass abound.

I found a patch where they do grow,
But tripped on roots—whoa, look at me go!
Covered in dirt, I struck a pose,
With berry juice dripping from my nose!

So here's the tale of berry bliss,
Each plump delight you cannot miss.
When life gives you fruit, squeeze it tight,
And laugh at the chaos, it feels just right!

Lush Landscapes of Delight

In a field of green, I danced with glee,
Twirled around like I was free.
But watch your step, oh what a plight,
A hidden berry, and I took flight!

A bounce and tumble, face first in a patch,
The neighbors laughed, what a fine catch!
With berry bits stuck in my hair,
I pondered life—was it all fair?

Each squishy bite was pure delight,
Yet my shirt now looked a scary sight.
A splash of juice, my pants do scream,
Fashion icon? Oh, that's the dream!

So here I stand, a berry beast,
Chasing sweets, never the least.
Join the fun or take a seat,
Life's more tasty with a fruity treat!

Tangy Tales from the Garden

I wandered out to pick a few,
Thought I was sly—oh how I blew!
A branch snapped back, it got me good,
Out came my shoe from where it stood.

The garden's secrets start to spill,
With every berry, I lose my will.
Tasting one, I grinned with glee,
But then I saw a mud-coated bee!

It buzzed around, I swatted high,
But instead it flew and made me cry.
My friends all roared, they couldn't see,
The real villain was slippery me!

So next time you brave the berry patch,
Watch each step, or you might hatch
A tale so wild, it can't be told,
Of tangy fruits and friendships bold!

Secrets Between Berry Vines

Between the vines, I found a nest,
A squirrel peeked out, oh what a jest!
He grabbed a berry with nimble paws,
I swear, it was breaking berry laws!

With a swift attack, he took a leap,
Leaving me laughing, my sides would keep.
I snatched one back, in playful rage,
Yet the squirrel howled, oh what a stage!

A battle ensued in our patchy land,
Who knew berries could be so grand?
Each chuckle echoed, a fruit-filled fight,
Secrets exchanged under the moonlight.

So when you wander the berry lane,
Expect some antics, a bit of pain.
With laughs and giggles, life's delight,
You'll find the fun is worth the bite!

Celebrating Nature's Confection

In the garden where laughter grows,
Berries burst like a joke, who knows?
With every nibble, giggles arise,
Nature's candy, a sweet surprise!

Red and round, they gleam with glee,
Wobbling softly, wild and free.
A berry dance on my tongue they start,
Tickling my taste buds, joy in each part!

Chasing petals, bees on a spree,
Biting bright fruit, just you and me.
With a punch of flavor, oh what fun!
A fruit-filled frenzy, we've just begun!

Gather round, let the fruit fight commence,
Strawberry puns are just too intense!
Taste buds delighted, hearts feeling bold,
Nature's confection, let the jokes unfold!

Elysium of Berry Fields

In fields of dreams, we frolic and play,
Berries laughing, brightening the day.
They wink and giggle, perched on their vines,
Juicy jesters in sweet sunshine shines!

Grandma once said, "Eat one, you'll float!"
I took a bite, and now I must gloat!
With berry juice dribbling down my chin,
Life's a riot, let the fun begin!

Red-robed jesters on a leafy throne,
Their fruity jokes will never be alone.
A splash of chuckles with every taste,
Berry laughter, we can't let it waste!

Sun-kissed fields where silliness reaps,
Tiny bites of fun, nature's sweet peeps.
Gather your friends, make a berry cheer,
In this fruity bliss, joy's ever near!

Sweet Kisses from Nature

A pink parade all lined in a row,
Nature's kisses, hear the laughter flow.
With every bite, a secret revealed,
Berry bliss from nature concealed!

Under the sun, they shimmer and sway,
Tickling noses in a most playful way.
Crisp and sweet, they dance on the tongue,
A giggle fest where the joy is sprung!

Tasting brightness from leafy cafes,
Flavors burst like jokes in a playful maze.
Who knew nature had such a knack?
For humor wrapped in berry-sweet snack!

From farm to table, laughter is shared,
With each tiny gem, we're utterly paired.
So grab a basket, let's fill it high,
Nature's humor under the wide-open sky!

Sunlit Mornings of Flavor

Morning light spills on the berry patch,
With every bite, we have a good match.
Sunlight giggles as it warms my cheek,
Berry laughter, sweet and chic!

Bright red gems twinkle with delight,
Tasting happiness, oh what a sight!
Nature's own candy, on fluffy toast,
I giggle and munch, loving it most!

Little bursts of joy, never a bore,
Dancing flavors, fruit galore!
With each delicious, sticky affair,
Funny faces with berry flair!

Escape with me as we berry dive,
Taste buds twirling, oh how we thrive!
In sunlit mornings where flavors collide,
Life's sweetest giggles are found inside!

Whimsical Fruit Adventures

In a patch so bright and bold,
Berries dance in stories told.
Hats of green, a sight to see,
Wiggle-waggle, oh, with glee!

Jellybeans join in the fun,
A giggle here, a pun to run.
Little ants march in a line,
Dreaming of a berry wine!

Pies that wiggle, cakes that prance,
Silly fruits do a silly dance.
Lemon voices sing a tune,
While cherries float beneath the moon!

So let's pick a feast tonight,
With berry bowls to our delight.
Laughter bubbles, friends agree,
In this fruity jubilee!

Starlit Nights in Juicy Melodies

Under stars, the fruits ignite,
Twinkling whispers, such delight!
Melons strum a joyful song,
While honeydews dance along.

Berries in a cabaret,
Raspberry twirls, a bright ballet.
Limes in tutus, oh so grand,
Inventing fun, hand in hand!

Tart companions, sweet brigade,
Sipping lemonade, a charade.
With every sip, giggles rise,
As juices flow with bright surprise!

Twilight's crunch, the laughter spreads,
As fruit salads bounce in beds.
Generous fun beneath the night,
Taste the joy, oh what a sight!

A Garden's Resplendent Gift

In the garden, laughter grows,
Berries sprout in silly rows.
Tomatoes wear a jaunty hat,
In bright parade, how about that?

Radishes prance with a cheeky grin,
While peas in pods do twist and spin.
Every veggie tells a tale,
Of mischief in the summer gale!

Golden carrots with a wink,
Silencing the thoughts that stink.
Zucchini friends, they roll and play,
In this leafy, bold cabaret!

So come and taste the garden's cheer,
Each bite brings laughter, that's for sure!
Celebrating in every dish,
Nature's gift, a humorous wish!

Heartfelt Offerings from Nature

A fruit bouquet, a funny sight,
With faces ripe, they feel just right.
Pinch the peaches, hear them squeak,
Witty fruits have quite the peak!

Grapes in hats, they giggle loud,
Twirling 'round, oh so proud.
Bananas slip with a vaudeville flair,
Charming all who stop and stare!

In this harvest, joy is king,
With every bite, our hearts take wing.
Plums and pears, mismatched socks,
Silly fruit plays, no time for clocks!

So gather round, let's have a feast,
Nature's bounty, to say the least.
Each heart rejoices in the yield,
This fruit-filled fun that nature healed!

Berry Dreams in Bloom

In a patch of red delight,
I stumbled on some berries bright.
They giggled with a fruity cheer,
Saying, "Eat us up! We're right here!"

With each bite of juicy bliss,
I couldn't help but steal a kiss.
They winked and jumped into my bowl,
"Don't you dare forget your role!"

I tossed them high, they soared so free,
"Catch us, catch us!" they squealed with glee.
A fruity fiesta under the sun,
Who knew that berries could be this fun?

So here's a toast with berry juice,
To the charm in each little moose.
Let laughter linger in the air,
With berries dancing everywhere!

Scarlet Treasures Unveiled

In the garden, a sneaky ploy,
Berries laughing like a toy.
They plotted schemes, oh what a sight,
To trick me into a berry fight!

With hats of leaf and juicy flair,
They rolled around without a care.
I chased them down, they took a spin,
Proclaiming, "You can't catch our grin!"

With giggles ripe, they popped and fizzed,
A berry party that was whizzed.
Cherries blushed and raspberries grinned,
In this sweet game, everyone wins!

So here I stand, with berry stains,
A jester here among these grains.
Let's dance around this berry mound,
Where scarlet treasures can be found!

Delicate Bliss in Each Bounty

In my garden, a gentle breeze,
Berries laughing among the trees.
I tiptoe softly, what a fright,
"Surprise!" they shout, "We're here for bite!"

With berry hats and charming flair,
They roll and tumble without care.
"Come join the fun, there's plenty to eat,
Our sweetness can't be beat!"

With sticky fingers and berry juice,
I can't resist this sweet excuse.
They twirled and laughed in pure delight,
"Be careful, friend, you've got a bite!"

I'm lost in bliss, a berry dream,
With every laugh, they're like a team.
Toast to the joy they bring each day,
What a wild, fruity ballet!

A Dance of Juicy Delights

Amidst the vines, a lively crew,
Berries jiving, just me and you.
They swing and sway in bright array,
"Join the dance, come here and play!"

With every twist, they burst with glee,
A berry band, just wait and see.
"On your toes!" they sing and shout,
"Groove with us, we're all about!"

I twirl and whirl, a comical sight,
Fruits in frolic under sunlight.
With laughter ringing in the air,
My struggles make them giggle and stare!

So let us dance, and sing with zest,
In this berry patch, we're truly blessed.
With juicy treats and lots of cheer,
Life's sweeter with friends so dear!

Savoring Moments Under the Sky

Under the sun, our laughter flies,
Juicy treasures, oh what a prize!
Caution thrown with every bite,
Dripping juice in sheer delight.

Found the berries, wild and free,
A game of hide and seek, you see!
Who knew they'd roll and skip away?
Chasing them, we laugh and play.

Sticky fingers, giggles loud,
We're the berry-loving crowd!
Creamy whims and sugar highs,
Moments captured, joy that flies.

As the sun dips down, we cheer!
One more scoop, let's split a tear.
Life's a feast under the blue,
Join us, won't you, for a chew?

The Aroma of Sunlit Euphoria

In a patch where sunshine gleams,
Plump and red, they burst with dreams.
Whimsical flavors, sweet and bold,
Our little adventures, worth their gold.

Bouncing berries, oh what fun!
Rolling down, they dare to run.
We catch them on this silly quest,
Who knew fruit could be such a jest?

Noses twitch, a fragrant breeze,
Spinning tales with berry tease.
One for you and two for me,
Vowing to share, but who can see?

Laughter echoes, the day completes,
Fruit-stained faces, laughter repeats.
Under the sun, tales are spun,
Forever young, still on the run.

Petals and Pools of Red

Petals dance beneath our feet,
A soft carpet, oh so sweet.
Berries blush, their ripe attire,
Come and join this berry choir.

More than fruit, they lie in wait,
A juicy trap, oh what a fate!
We dive into this berry bliss,
Who can resist? Just one more kiss!

Squishy treats, oh the delight!
Chasing berries, what a sight!
A marathon of sweet delight,
We giggle 'til the fall of night.

Twirling in the summer air,
Stomach aches from too much care.
In our world, we laugh and sing,
Berry mischief is our thing!

Butterflies and Berry Baskets

Basket full of giggles bloom,
Running wild, no need for gloom.
Butterflies dance, we chase them too,
How many berries? Just a few!

Juggling fruit, oh what a feat!
Splashing juice makes it all sweet.
Each red gem hides a surprise,
Biting in, oh what a prize!

We create a berry brigade,
In the patch, a playful trade.
Swapping colors, sweet and round,
Loud laughter is the only sound.

As daylight fades, our hearts unswayed,
With berry follies, memories made.
Under stars, we'll reminisce,
Butterfly dreams, we seal with bliss.

Whispers of a Sugary Breeze

In fields where giggles gently sway,
Juicy gems hide from sunlight's play.
Bouncing bees wear tiny hats,
Chasing dreams as they sip on sprats.

Worms have parties, plotting their schemes,
Berries blush while laughing at their dreams.
Sunshine dances, tickling the air,
Plants gossip with flair beyond compare.

A frolicsome breeze whispers sweet tunes,
As ants wear shades, grooving with raccoons.
Laughter erupts like a fizzy drink,
Who knew fruits could cause such a wink?

In a world where flavor reigns supreme,
Each bite is a giggle, a sugary dream.
So grab your hats, and sing a fun song,
For in this berry land, we all belong.

Essence of Summer on the Palate

With every bite, a burst of cheer,
Fruity shenanigans draw us near.
The squirrels, they dance, a summer ballet,
While chipmunks toast, come what may.

Jars of jam fit for a king,
Made by critters who've got the swing.
They mix, they giggle, they stir with flair,
While the sun paints warm colors everywhere.

On sun-soaked days, the laughter flies,
Pies cooling off, amidst the cries.
The taste of summer hangs in the air,
Like a juicy secret, a delicious dare.

So laugh with us in this fruity delight,
Where berries reign, and everything's bright.
With every nibble, a smile does bloom,
In the land of sweetness, there's always room.

Crimson Delights

In a garden where giggles spill free,
Crimson wonders hang from each tree.
A frog in a hat sings to a bee,
While squirrels play tag as happy as can be.

Munching our way through red, round charms,
Tickling taste buds with fruity alarms.
With spoons in hand, and smiles so wide,
Who knew fruit could be such a fun ride?

A jam session rocks on a pie-plate stage,
The fruits all dance, unleashing their rage.
Plump and ripe, they take the floor,
While ants in tuxedos come in for more.

So if you're seeking a berry retreat,
Join the laughter with a fruity treat.
In a land where sweetness plays all day,
Each taste a giggle, come join the fray!

Berry Bliss Beneath the Sun

Under the sun, we laugh and munch,
Each berry plucked is a giggly punch.
Beetles rock out to a jammin' tune,
While fruit flies boogie beneath the moon.

Ripe red fruits call out with glee,
Come taste the fun, just trust me!
With every nibble, a smirk will grow,
As laughter spills like a sweetened flow.

Giggly picnics spread on the ground,
With splashes of cream, joy knows no bound.
Berry wars start as splats take flight,
A snack-time battle that feels so right.

So throw down your cares, bring your spoon,
Join the fiesta, watch the berries croon.
In this fun-filled patch, we roam and run,
For there's happiness ripe under the sunny fun!

Savoring Morning's Ruby Light

In the garden where mischief grows,
Berries giggle in morning rows.
They wiggle and waggle, a berry parade,
Sunshine gleams on their gourmet shade.

With a basket in hand, I brace for the race,
Chasing the fruit, it's a berry good chase!
One bounces, then rolls, it's quite a sight,
'Catch me if you can,' it calls with delight.

Plump and juicy, they tease my tongue,
Each tart bite feels like a song that's sung.
A raspberry whisper, oh what a joke!
They crack all the puns, and then take a poke.

With every nibble, I giggle and snort,
Dancing with joy, a fruity retort.
With my mouth full, I ponder the bliss,
Who knew berries could taste like sheer happiness?

Sprints of Joy in the Orchard

In a patch of green, I've made my stand,
Berries bouncing, oh, isn't it grand?
They play tag with bees and hide from the sun,
Sprinting through vines, oh what silly fun!

One popped up, said, "Bet you can't catch!"
I stumbled and fumbled right into a patch.
With laughter as loud as a tractor's loud horn,
Fruits high-fived me, how could I be worn?

A berry brigade in a fruity fleet,
Leading a march to the sun's warm seat.
They laugh and they dance, oh what a sight!
Even squirrels join in, under the light.

Juicy treasures in every crate,
They wink and they laugh, oh, isn't this fate?
With sticky fingers and a smile so wide,
I'll drink to this chaos and joy-filled ride!

Ripened Kisses at Dawn

Morning sun, the petals dance,
Ants in line, they steal a glance.
Each red bulb, a cheeky tease,
Sweetened whimsies on the breeze.

Birds are chirping, gossip flies,
While squirrels plot, oh such wise spies.
A berry fight? Who'll take the prize?
With sticky fingers, laughter cries.

Mornings greet with juicy bites,
Friends in tow for silly sights.
Giggles burst like bubbles pop,
Juicy drops, can't let them stop!

With laughter shared 'neath leafy crowns,
They're sweet mischiefs, wearing frowns.
Every taste a playful jest,
In this orchard, we're the best!

Velvet Juices on the Tongue

A tiny feast, oh what delight,
Velvet plumpness in their sight.
Go ahead, take another bite,
Giggle fits, oh pure delight!

Sticky hands and berry stains,
Ticklish feels, like summer trains.
Juice drips down, it calls your name,
Oh what fun in this sweet game!

Paths of red and paths of fun,
In the sun, we start to run.
Chasing blooms with laughter loud,
Berry lovers, oh so proud!

With every taste, a twist in fate,
Turning cheeks to bright estate.
Ripe suggestions in the air,
Crafty tricks with daring flair!

Berry Whispers of Summer

In fields of green, we scamper round,
Berry whispers, joyful sound.
Silly pranks from toes to head,
Sweet mischiefs in the berry bed.

Sunshine giggles, laughter swirls,
Worms tell tales, a garden whirls.
Strawberry dreams, we taste and twirl,
Giggling cats with tails that curl.

Pick a handful, share a grin,
Fairy friends in this wild spin.
Juicy dribble, silly faces,
Life is sweeter in these places!

Spinning 'round with berry joy,
Crafty schemes, we all employ.
Nature's treats, oh what a score,
In this summer, we adore!

Crimson Gems in the Orchard

Crimson gems upon the vine,
Whispers of joy, oh so divine.
Squirrels plotting, what a show,
Each red treasure, play and glow.

Dancing shadows, giggles burst,
Picking berries, oh what thirst!
Laughter spills, a friendly fight,
Who can taste the juiciest right?

Jars in hand, we race the sun,
Magic moments, so much fun.
Splatters everywhere, a fruity art,
In this orchard, we'll never part!

Summer skies and berry cheer,
Whirling dreams when friends are near.
Every mouthful sings a tune,
As cheeky laughter fills the noon!

Nectar Drips from Lushness

In a patch of green, they gleam bright,
Red little gems, a comical sight.
With every bite, a squirt and a dash,
Someone's shirt is now a sticky splash!

Gather 'round, the feast begins,
With helmets on, avoiding sins.
Laughter echoes through the bright sun,
As fruity antics have just begun!

Outrun the bees, they zippity-dash,
While plucking berries with giggles and laughs.
A bumpy ride on a berry-filled cart,
Who knew sugar could bring such art?

Rolling in patches, so light on our feet,
Picking up juice like a summer retreat.
Share a wink with the ladybug crew,
In the garden, foolishness grew!

Scarlet Echoes in the Garden

In the garden, where whispers play,
The fruit are plotting in a berry ballet.
With laughter ripe on a sunny day,
Berry jokes are the game they portray!

A berry brigade, all dressed in red,
Joking about what the farmer said.
'If you eat too many, you'll turn to juice!'
The puns just flow, no sign of truce!

Marshmallow clouds float above the blooms,
While berry lovers invade with their spoons.
Chasing each other, but none keep the score,
As juice wars erupt—oh, what a chore!

Under the sun, they dance and twirl,
Sweet sticky chaos in a fruity whirl.
In this garden, laughter'll unfold,
With stories that never grow old!

Flavors of Forgotten Days

Once upon a time, in a berry patch,
A squirrel conversed with a tomato hatch.
They shared tales of flavors so wild,
With giggles that could make the sun feel mild!

Racing for a taste, they jumped in pairs,
Landing in mud, with wild berry flares.
Nothing beats the jest of the past,
Where days were funny and friendships vast!

Jellybeans stuck to a sticky old shoe,
In this adventure, nothing feels new!
With raucous laughter and messy delight,
Who needs dinner when dessert's in sight?

At twilight, the flavors fill the air,
Goofy memories are beyond compare.
So raise a toast to the sweetness we crave,
For in silly moments, we always behave!

Joyful Sips of Fruity Dreams

In a blender's whirl, the fun begins,
Fruit splashes everywhere, oh what spins!
Mixing with laughter, a chaotic blend,
Sipping dreams, with smiles that extend.

A twist of the cap—oh no, what a splash!
Fruits everywhere, a berryish bash!
Friends in a frenzy, look at that mess,
With joyful giggles, we feel truly blessed!

Slurping and swirling, what flavors unite,
In this fruity tornado, we dance with delight.
What would we do without berry crunch?
Every sip brings us closer for lunch!

So gather around, let's blend some cheer,
Shake up memories, let's toast with a beer!
In every drop, our laughter streams,
Toasting life with our fruity dreams!

Sweetness in Every Bite

A berry burst of joy, oh what a delight,
I took a big bite, then lost my sight!
With juice on my chin and a grin so wide,
These little treasures are a wild ride.

I raced with my friends, we dashed and we splashed,
Tripping on vines, how we laughed and we crashed!
One berry too many, my belly's so round,
Good thing no one here is wearing a crown.

Plump red jewels hanging, oh what a sight,
Should I eat them all, or just take a bite?
The laughter is loud, the juice hits my shoe,
If only you knew the berry-licious view!

So here is my tale of berry-filled fun,
With sun on my face and the day nearly done.
I'll prance down the lane with a smile so bright,
Life is too short, so let's eat and take flight!

A Symphony of Berry Notes

In the garden's heart, a concert erupts,
Berry tunes dancing, and anyone interrupts!
Fiddles and laughter in the creamy sunbeam,
Who knew fruit could play such a silly dream?

A berry brass band with raucous delight,
Plucking and strumming, it's quite the sight!
Allergies tingle, my nose starts to sneeze,
Butchering notes like a buzzing bee's wheeze.

They sing of the sweetness, the tart and the ripe,
The thumping of berries, it's quite the hype!
One berry took flight, directly on cue,
And splattered my hat, just to say "How do you do?"

The music keeps bumping, let's burst into song,
Forget about calories, just dance along!
With berries as buddies, let's savor the day,
This fruity symphony's here to stay!

Petals, Leaves, and Berry Thieves

In a field of joy where the berries do sway,
A squirrel plots mischief, as bold as the day.
With petals and leaves, he dashes about,
Whisking away treasures with a little berry shout!

He nibbles and munches, a feisty fox friend,
Together they scheme, plotting fruity mayhem to blend.
A pirouette here, a dash and a roll,
Oh, berry bandits, they're on a roll!

But wait, here comes Daisy, bright-eyed and keen,
With sunscreen and laughter, she can intervene!
With a sprinkle of giggles and a banana peel,
The thieves take a tumble, the berry caper's real!

A dance of delight, a berry-filled spree,
Who knew fruit thieves were such fun to see?
Forest friends laughing, they sip and they chew,
In a berry patch world, it's all about the view!

Sunlit Orchard Serenade

In the orchard so bright, where laughter takes flight,
Sunshine spills over, a sweet, wondrous sight.
Jubilant chortles, the air filled with cheer,
As we dodge around rows of berries, oh dear!

Swinging on swings made of garden twine,
One berry unleashed, flew right past the line.
With gooey green globes and a sweet melon ball,
We giggle and tumble, just having a ball!

The sunshine then winks, as I hug a tree,
A splash of berry juice; oh, it's got to be me!
A sticky situation, but laughter is grand,
As we all join together in this funny berry band.

With baskets now filled and our giggles in bloom,
The orchard serenades with a fruity perfume.
Under blue skies, we sing without shame,
In this berry-filled paradise, we've made our own fame!

Harvesting Daydreams

In the garden where giggles grow,
Red gems hang, putting on a show.
I reach for one, it jumps away,
Turns out it's just my buddy's play.

With baskets wide, we plot and scheme,
Plucking dreams, or so it seems.
One for me and one for you,
Oops! I ate the whole damn crew!

The sun is bright, the laughs are loud,
Nature's treat makes us so proud.
We dress in hats, as silly as can be,
A fashion show for birds—you'll see!

As we giggle, the juice does flow,
A sticky mess, a fruity glow.
Under the sun, we dance and roll,
Harvesting dreams while munching whole.

Serendipity in a Strawberry Field

In a field so lush, we run amok,
With berry stains like punk rock shock.
My hat flies off, a rogue on the breeze,
Looks like a squirrel's cooking up his tease.

What's that? A berry wearing shades?
Laughing at us as the daylight fades.
We trip over vines, bounce like fools,
Eating our treasure, breaking all rules.

I spotted a red, I took a bite,
But it turned out to be a bug's delight.
We scream, we yell, oh what a sight,
Turns out it's dinner on a strawberry night!

With hands so sticky, we make a pact,
To create the wildest berry snack.
But as we giggle and indulge our fate,
Who knew fruit could be so first-rate!

Sweetness Between the Rows

Between the rows, we sneak and peek,
With sneaky smiles and giggles unique.
I spotted one, so plump and round,
But it rolled away, and I'm on the ground!

Our farmer friend comes down the way,
With a warning not to munch and play.
But there's laughter in this fruity spree,
As we fill our faces and climb a tree.

Under the sun, a sticky affair,
We turn bright red; it's a berry dare.
Each berry picked brings squeals of joy,
A strawberry ninja, not just a boy!

The day drips sweet, our shirts are stained,
But with every bite, we feel unchained.
With each laugh shared, oh what a scene,
We're sticky bandits, berry-lovin' machine!

A Symphony of Red Delights

In a world of red, oh what a song,
Guitar strings plucking, berry sweet throng.
Each berry pulled, like notes that rise,
A symphony played 'neath sunny skies.

A jam session starts, with drums of mess,
A squishy berry makes for a big guess.
We clap and cheer, what a wild beat,
Dancing in dirt with sticky feet!

In harmony of laughter, we all unite,
With giggles and bites, the mood's just right.
A berry to share, here comes a race,
But now I'm stuck in a berry embrace!

The finale comes with splashes and spills,
We laugh and roll down grassy hills.
With every taste, this tune we write,
A fruity symphony, pure delight!

Moments Caught in Sweetness

In a garden bright, they dance with glee,
Little critters munching, oh what a spree!
Juicy rubies tucked beneath the leaves,
Laughter echoes softly, a joy that weaves.

Silly squirrels tumble, their cheeks so round,
Chasing each other, joyfully they bound.
A berry feast planned, but chaos is near,
Who knew fruit hunting could bring such cheer?

Sticky fingers poke, oh what a sight,
A family picnic, all day and night.
Giggles erupt as juice flies anew,
Delightfully messy, just me and you.

In this sweet patch of nature's delight,
Every berry harvest feels oh so right.
With laughter and smiles, we share our finds,
Moments caught in sweetness, forever binds.

Nature's Whimsy on a Plate

Oh, look at that berry, perched on my fork,
It giggles and wiggles, like it's a dork!
With whipped cream hats and chocolate dust,
Nature's own treat, and oh how we trust!

The napkins are ready, the plates piled high,
Berry juice rivers, oh my, oh my!
With laughter that bubbles like fizzy sweet soda,
Every bite's a party, nature's fine quota!

Watch out for the seeds, they sneakily hide,
In a battle of flavors, we take it in stride.
Daring each other to take a big bite,
Nature's whimsy, oh what a sight!

The picnic unfolds with a fantastical flair,
Berries and laughter hang thick in the air.
To taste every giggle, that's truly the goal,
Nature's own whimsy, feeding the soul.

Gems of Summer Melodies

Under the sun, in shades of delight,
Berries sing songs, all juicy and bright.
Pick one for me, and don't you forget,
It's nature's own jam, a glorious duet.

The ants throw a party, or so it would seem,
Trying to steal a sweet berry dream.
While honeybees buzz with a busy little hum,
Gems of summer melodies, here they come!

Oh look, there's a blueberry, bold and round,
Dancing on cookies, it's quite the crown!
A fruity brigade, we savor each slice,
Giggles and grins, oh, this will suffice.

So do take a fork, or a spoon if you dare,
But don't blame the berries for getting you smeared.
Gems of summer, oh what a spree,
In joy and in laughter, forever we'll be!

Peeking into Berry Treasures

What's hiding in bushes, so sweet and divine?
A world of surprises, a berry shrine!
With mischief and giggles, let's embark on a quest,
Peeking into treasures, we'll find the best!

Oh, watch that berry thief, with hurry and haste,
Nibbling and munching, oh, what a waste!
Sticky trails follow, like candy on toes,
Nature's adventure and laughter grows.

Pickles and berries in a curious mix,
What odd combinations can we conjure up quick?
S silliness reigns as we dive deep in,
The treasure chest's open, it's laughter we win!

So take your big bowl, and fill it with cheer,
For every last berry brings laughter near.
Peeking into treasures, with smiles that last,
With fruity adventures, we're having a blast!

www.ingramcontent.com/pod-product-compliance
Lightning Source LLC
Chambersburg PA
CBHW060123230426
43661CB00003B/309